The Woman I Hold Dear

The Woman I Hold Dear

Amber Campbell

ORANGE
R O S E
PRESS

Other Books by Amber Campbell

The Ones

Missed Arrows

Daughter of the Bottle

For the women who built me
and continue to shape me.

Table of Contents

Woman

Hibernation by any other name

When the yellow leaves float to the chipped asphalt
Of the pothole-riddled street behind my house,
I will rise from them and put myself first.
Spring breathes life into the earth,
Summer unleashes ease and work under the sun,
And autumn ushers in quietude among its reddish hues.
But winter silences the quake in my bones
And lays my quivering muscles to rest,
For if the earth is allowed three months to die,
Then surely, too, am I.

My brain knows the truth of my heart,
But my mouth refuses to speak of it.
My body understands the roots of its people,
But my spirit yearns for loneliness in Nantucket.
I once dreamed of spending a winter
Among the snow, and dark, and solitude,
But faced laughter from my friends,
For how would I survive without interaction?
Because I had my stories to keep me company,
Writing on the walls and on the floors
And within the flames of a hearth.
Before the digital proximity of everything at once
Around nothing at all, waiting for
A ping, a call, a reminder that someone far
From me relishes my commentary.
I'm convinced I will only find true companionship
Within a cottage in the snowy wilderness,
My bones to hold me and my mind to speak.
No greater contentment could I seek.

Can I bury this family heirloom?

My inner critic must be short on rent
If the overtime he's putting in gives an indication.
I question how our pain transforms us
But refuses to leave, scarring the skin
Until the hope of fading fades.
How do I forfeit the monster in my chest
And free my soul from the torment
That you never intended to give?
Is the anger for myself and my naivety?
Is the rage for all women who tasted betrayal
That still burns on their tongues like cheap whiskey?
When did my self-control spiral down the same road
That my fear begged me to never follow?

Rock to Resin

I draped capes over stillwater,
And you leapt into the puddles
With the enthusiasm of a toddler
But the force of a queen,
Soaking me worse than our
Sandy soil had ever seen.
I vowed to be your rock,
To hold you steady in the storm,
But these coups left so many wounds
I can no longer keep you warm.
I am a rock by nature,
But my birthright is preservation,
And I will burn down every structure
These lowlifes constructed
To provide you with every ounce of nurture
Until your tender heart is sure.

I want to be enough

A thousand apologies cannot salvage
The whirlwind storm of rage
That fills my body when I remember
How my actions only made you bitter
Because I was meant to be greater
Than the fury of the past. Your sage wisdom
Fights well enough but cannot wage
A proper war against everything
That stops me from being the person
Who stops your tears from falling.
Teach me how to desire each tomorrow
When I'm the reason for your every sorrow.

It Others You

The mouths that whisper my problems
Are the ears who listened as I confessed
To all the ways I was broken.
The pity I received from the ones I confided
Is harder to endure than the pain of silence.
That's why I don't tell people.
It others you.

On Waiting

Everyone's having babies
And getting married when they still
Resemble children in my eyes.
I was an old maid at the golden year
Of twenty-eight when I wed.
No human young to my name,
But a new moniker to claim
To ease the burden no one warns of
When life paints a portrait unimagined.
The news buried itself deep in my chest
When I realized I'd only be blessed
With little sets of babes I left
In the ground, in the sky, and in the tears wept
After saying goodbye. But I still feel them
In the ache in my bones and in the emptiness
Of my womb on nights when I hear
The wind howl like a newborn's cry.

At the ripe old age of nine, I wrote in my future biography (whatever the hell that entailed) that I wouldn't be married because I was stupid and ugly. My fourth-grade teacher, a woman who was often pregnant, thought the best method to teach my childish heart was to ask me how I would feel if my children one day found this and read it.

No positive talk of body view. No questions asking why I viewed myself as worthless as if something could have been going on at home or in her godforsaken classroom of mean boys. Only arguments of children I decided I didn't want at the ripe old age of nine, but I had enough wisdom to not speak my true feelings out loud. What would a woman know of girlhood?

I couldn't have known then, still a few years from my menstruation, that conceiving would be near impossible. I couldn't have known that the man I would marry had been burned by women as he cared for children he didn't father. I couldn't have known that I couldn't handle children because of my depression and chronic pain.

But there I was, nine years old, expecting to think of the children God said I couldn't have until he stole the breath back from my body and met them above. No one ever told my husband to think of his children because men have more important things to consider, like their work, interests, and vices. It's not a man's job to concern himself with children he'll never carry.

But to have a woman tell me to think of my children? To have a person whom I should have felt safe to confide in with whatever fucked up problem I was going through inform me that I was wrong for thinking of myself first before people who would never exist?

You're right, Mrs. Norton. How dare I think of myself. For the next thirteen years, my body and mind will never again cross from my pen to paper, because as you'd point out, these words and the books they create aren't my children. But I'll be damned if they're not my babies.

Accept my sincerest of apologies,
Women who wear their wrinkles with pride,
Ladies who treasure wisdom above experience.
I knew not what I still know not now,
But I see well to know I need your guidance.
The youth of adulthood pales
Beside the elegance of your thin skin
And deep-set laugh lines I once perceived
As a sign of life since passed.
A woman may be defined after blood spills,
But the women I look up to have dried wombs.
They have maneuvered the chaos of this world
To grant patience to pistols like me,
Who once chased ambition in the masculine lens.
But I faltered and angered and seethed in my inefficacy
Until I discovered my feminine power
To collect my thoughts, calm my heart,
Listen to my soul, and breathe with my being.
My thirties feature a far wiser woman
Than my previous decade could have fathomed,
And I welcome in the age of the old woman
As the last remaining era I will ever seek.

The woman I hold dear

She quotes Dickinson and dissects Plath,
She reads of minds greater than mine,
But she can't read a room.

As a child, I never understood my mother's driving force
Behind cleaning the dishes and wiping the counters
And vacuuming the carpet and reorganizing the cabinets
When my father raised his voice a little too loudly.
The chore I dreaded with youthful immaturity
Became my solace when my thoughts raged
Louder than the freight train that barreled through
Every Tuesday and Friday at 4:27 a.m.
I couldn't quiet the transportation that shook the house
Or silence the regrets scheming in my ears,
But I could ignore it all when the burn of the water
Scorched my fingers like a wildfire.
I controlled the soap burying itself underneath
My short nails and the force of the spout
As it rinsed off the day's crunchy reminders.
I washed away the grime of my soul
And waved as it spiraled down the drain.
I couldn't temper the torrential soundwaves
That pelted my memories and shook me to my core
Years after therapy taught me to listen to their cries,
But now their curses lament into soft whispers
That tickle my brain but not my rage.
I focus on the sparrow outside the window,
Wondering if it's better to not know of cleaning as an anchor
Than to never appreciate a moment to stop the chatter
And listen to the banter of a brown and white singer.
I clean the dishes even when the sink is empty.

Brush of ocean

A brush of ocean across my body
Reminds me of the saltwater kisses
That summoned me to the edge
Of the beach, sand between every crevice,
Inviting me back to the world that birthed me.
What is it about nature
That calls to womanhood so boldly?
The oceans sway with the womb I carry
And the babe it won't conceive.
The forests envelope me in cool safety,
While the mountains rise above me
And straighten my back to match
The majesty of the hard rock and powdered browns.
The sun and moon cat-and-mouse
My heart and brain, neither winning,
Bobbing and swimming in the ebb and
Flow of the saltwater that caresses
And reminds me I am always home with her.

Worry steeps my brain each evening I sit to write
Another piece about heartbreak and anger,
And I fear my emotions on paper more than
I fear any literary criticism of the structure.
It must tie in to how women are chained to the idea
Of marriage and children and homesteading,
But we're ridiculed by men for only writing sad poems
About our love lives as if they ever provided
An alternative to our lives or the disappointing
Relationships they meekly offer.
My womanhood contains all the parts of me
And every woman who has walked this earth,
And each one is tainted by a man who told her
How she should be if she wants to be loved.
And yet our mothers and grandmothers demanded
That we speak our voice and hide from violence,
And a woman has never told me to quiet my energy
To allow hers to shine. But a man expects it.
The men of today fail to comprehend what we desire.
We beg to be equals in work and home,
But within the graces of our feminine energy
Because we can be women who command the stage
While representing the power bestowed unto us
Because God determined men couldn't handle both.
We are two sides of the same coin:
Steely, strong, valued, but you would never dare
Be caught playing with a quarter without a head.
I will stop writing sad poetry
When you stop objectifying me.

Blow into the breeze, gray as grief,
And shed your cloak of silence.
No longer will we cling to forbidden whispers
That threaten to mold us into ideas softer
Than the greatness we hide from in the dark.
The story is never finished
Until the breath seeps from our bodies,
So close the chapter on the losses
We still shove into our dressers with tear-stained
Photographs and wisps of their voices,
Even though the lilt eludes our ears
From far too many nights apart.
Step into the midnight of a new day,
Quiet, free, soaked in solace,
And tasting of the sweetest food
On which we have yet to indulge.

Warden

Rust by the wayside

Pristine as marble and just as breakable
Despite the facade addressed by your frown.
Whiskers of gray freckle your chin
Where once vibrant strands of black
Contrasted against your chiseled, sunburnt skin.

Sharp as uncut diamond and just as splintered
Before you rehearsed every line you spoke.
An actor on a stage bowing to performances that
I relived every encore in a food-stained dress
Till the applause deafened me to sleep and bitter dreams.

Tough as steel and just as perceptible
To the elements as your love to your attitude.
The silver, sleek exterior shattered in time,
Rust by the wayside like the foxing of the pages
Of the romances I believed you'd one day remember.

Memorable as murder and just as messy
When the axe of your words ripped my flesh.
Torched by ice, melted by flames,
Reality spun on the axis of an unknown plane
When you stole our story from my breath.

Wrapped in hushed moments and soft embraces,
Touched with the hands of an angel
And the burn of a forest fire.
You engulfed my fears in the hazy white light
That emanated from your eyes when you soliloquized
And scorched my tongue with a feathery kiss
All in the name of something not quite love
But nothing I've experienced since.
The stars spell your name and the wind howls it—
The sand slips through my fingers back to yours
In a way that's not quite love
But something that can never be enough.

My heart beats for the blood in my veins,
But my soul aches for a lost embrace
And a glimpse of the slight smile that graced your face
Each time your eyes caught sight
Of my hands out the window, reaching for the sky,
Believing in a love within a cocooned lie.
If a white lie is meant to protect a heart,
Then yours would have been more blinding
Than the universe at its start,
A creation more dazzling than a work of art,
A love in the palm that never felt more far
Than when it held my cheek in the dark,
Whispering promises behind a dive bar.

False dreams

I was the girl of your dreams,
But you've woken up, it seems.
Our love ran out of steam
The moment you realized I was me.

Of angels and demons

The angel on my shoulder
Ran off with the devil
Because it couldn't deliver salvation
From the hell you held in your hands
Each time you held my name on your lips.
All I'm left with is my humanity
That's too naive to understand
How it finds goodness
In people undeserving of a chance.

The anger on your breath when I refuted your friendship burns my ears now as it did then. Did you not see the anguish in my hard-lined lips? Could you not hear the tremor in my heartbeats as the thought of a new woman on your arm flitted across my mind? Betrayal etched in the wrinkles around your eyes, but the betrayal that ate at me never crossed your mind.

"If we separated, I'd still be your friend."

How naive. I never imagined a man of your status would remain so youthful. What use did I have of what-ifs and promises after? If you loved me with the breath in your lungs, the thought would never have uttered into words from your mouth. You loved the version of yourself you could be with me, but instead of transforming into the pretty little thing you carried on your arm to flaunt to your barmates, I begged you to perform your duty as a man.

"How could you turn your back on me so easily?"

I fought for your reputation without understanding how each battle waged a war on mine, burying my worth deeper underground. I stood up to my family when they saw through your ruse, tarnishing relationships I'd be nothing without. I struggled to mark myself as the woman of your life, but you demoted me to nothing more than a girl in your story. I was the mistake you made too permanent.

"Maybe we'll be together in another life."

Or maybe this isn't the first lifetime we've shared. Maybe this was the thirty-third encounter and each life, our relationship ends just a few days sooner. Perhaps in the next life, I won't bother tying myself to people who see me as the back-up plan, their prized second best. Perhaps in the next life, I won't entertain the approach of a desperate man in a bar who only had an interest in a pretty stupid thing for his reputation's security.

I was once your reality. Now I'm a memory that your next life would be wise to forget.

You read me like a crossword clue,
Paint my numbers royal blue,
Fill in my sudoku with ones and twos,
Convinced unlocking the puzzles will evolve
Into a person you no longer need to solve.
But there was nothing for you to fix.
The thought made you sick,
All your effort so valiantly wasted
As I showed my cards in their counterfeit.
Your paper games skills came undone
Under the unspeakable icosahedron
That makes up the pieces of my soul that none
Had been able to unravel and tie into one.
I'm sorry to apologize, but the fault isn't mine
That you struggled for all that time
Over pieces of a heart instead of striving to find
How your pieces fit into my design.

Melancholic Kisses

Sometimes I still feel
The dilaudid in my veins,
And I lie through my teeth
When I say I feel the same
As I did before the understanding
Drowned my beliefs and sank them
Deep into the ocean floor,
The layer we haven't discovered yet.
The one we haven't yet learned to fear.
I want to be someone you never forget,
But I know I'll only be the one you regret.

Broken muse

Did you love my poetry?
Or did you love that a piece
Of me would always be near?
Tucked into your back pocket,
A sheet of paper in your wallet,
A reminder that you alone
Were always on my mind.
Did you love me in my entirety,
Broken bones and broken spirit,
Or did you love the idea
Of being my muse? Memorialized
In someone's torn book, pages
Dog-eared and coffee-stained. Years have
Passed, my questions no use,
But still my heart asks
Why you didn't stay,
And why I never asked you to.

Whimsy adorns your eyes, starlight.
Piercing through the darkest alleys, I sought
The glow that could cloud my bitter judgment
Because we both know love is nothing more
Than overlooking the pain we'll inflict
When our traumas outweigh us.
The pull of societal expectations
Mean nothing against an orange-hued streetlight
On a snowy evening when a snowflake
Catches on my eyelash, and your mittened-hand
Whisks it away, nothing but a breath in between,
But you're further away than you've ever been.
Remember when we raced between houses
Coming home from school in fifth grade?
You hung up the fairy lights in our treehouse
And you chased off the other boys
When they laughed and called you names.
The fire in your eyes that day matches
The light in my chest when you hold me,
And each night you catch me laughing in your arms.
Your gentle smile against my cheek repeats
The same whimsy we embraced in our youth.
My dear starlight, never fade, but if you
Explode into a dazzling display of cosmic dust,
I know your glittering goodbye
Will be my final touch of wanderlust.

Golden child, meet eldest daughter

No one worries for the golden child.
No one worries for the eldest daughter.
They are the backbone of the household,
Neither a leader nor a ward, but the straw
That refuses to break the family's backs.
How many nights must be spent alone,
Fearful of revealing the weakness in her bones?
How many days must be Fly and Save
For those who remain unaware of the grave
She dug as a child to prepare her loved ones
For her goodbye when she's finally done?
Even in death, the eldest daughter must protect
Her family's hearts from breaking at the inevitable onset
Of realizing everything they bore on her shoulders
Was never the love she needed to stay golden.

New, wax, full, wane

Seven years.
Seven years my body will be transformed.
New cells, new skin, new parts of my body
You have never seen or touched,
And I will break free of the mental torment
Of the bruised markings.
I will rip off the tattoos
I once thought were proof
That I had understood a bitter man's truth,
And I will fully embrace the changes I undergo
To become a woman untainted by you.
My heart wanes, not with longing,
But with regret and shame,
But it, too, will be washed away.
The cycle is nearly complete.

The burden weighs across my back,
Weakened from years of labor blind
To you, and the lack of concern is kinder
Than the falsities you feed with a laced
Smile that stretches your skin too thin.
May I now breathe? May I now rest?
May I remove your head from my chest
So that my lungs will refill with the air
You stole from my mouth with a kiss
So sour it puckered my lips.
May I now stop? May I now close my eyes
And lay down my head and touch
A body you don't own?
Hear my pleas and heed my warnings.
Neither are in good or wayward faith. May
I now live a life for the little girl who
Forfeited herself when she forged a new path.
May I now breathe? May I please rest?

The warden ran off; call the dogs

I splintered your arm, iced your wrist,
Covered you in blankets amidst
A blizzard of cold hearts and cruel wits,
And I froze by the broken heater
That you always did mean to fix.
Did you ever expect to meet her?
The woman who warmed your bitterness
Better than the emotional mess
Of me and my questions that always perplexed
Your wiser ways of how a woman ought to be.
I can't correct my mask because your vexed
Words sliced me deeper than a rusty shank.
I cared for you, protected you from the world,
But I was the one trapped in the cell.
You made a prisoner of your warden, and then
Had the audacity to cry abandonment
When I found the key and escaped your jail.
When does a warden feel the freedom
Of someone dutifully providing for them?
I'd love to be the one behind bars
If it meant I didn't have to bleed out.
I'm repeating myself, but the walls don't mind.
It seems all they have is time.

Wife

Tender

I built a stone wall around the ashes
Because the warmth kept me alive
After the stake stopped smoldering.
But instead of tearing down the bricks,
You wrapped me in blankets and gave me time
To heal myself before I learned your name.
You tended to my torn skin like a gardener
To a bloom: delicately, tenderly, adoringly,
As though I'd wilt under too much compassion.
You watered and tilled my stagnant ground
Until I towered above you and sprouted new buds.
My roots tore through the stone around us,
And nature overtook the humanity I clung to.
The sun no longer burned but shone.
The rain no longer flooded but cleansed.
The petals flourished in shades of red, pink, and orange,
Hues of my namesake painting your skin
As I showered you in velvety petals of my better self.
I never needed someone to put me back together.
I needed someone to mind to the world around me
While I saved myself, and only your tenderness
Could bring me back while clinging to you
And everything we represent together.
Our souls meshed on a bed of roses.

Fireworks lit the sky when you kissed me,
And I swore they rained down sparks that seared my arms.
The reds, blues, and yellows against a black night
Drowned us in muted primaries,
And I'll chase that high my whole life.
You found my scars and erased them with your lips.
I found the internal bleeding and sewed you together
With nothing but my fingertips.
We'd only known love that burned and drowned us,
But within our wounds we fished out the salt
And let the rain soak us to the bone
Until the water and lightshow crafted a waterfall of fire
That burned everyone around us.

Tell me what you thought
The first time your eyes caught mine.
Did I shine like a ray on a dark night?
Did I draw you in like a moth to a flame?
Did you turn away out of shyness
Or of fear of what could be the end?
Did you wonder what I loved to spend
My quiet evenings doing, and if
You might enjoy them, too?
Did you want to whisk me away
To a corner of the room
Where you could command all my attention
As if you didn't already hold it?
I long to know every thought that entails me,
To understand the depths you sought me,
To know if I'm chasing a dream
Or finally clutching my destined reality.

Daybreak

The dawn awakens the truth
I hid under the sheets and between our pillows.
The dusk lulls my fears because longing
Can't exist when I'm in your arms,
But the sunrise pulls me away before the world
Learns that two lost souls found a shred of hope
In the safety of the stars.

Wasteland hearts

Your velvety touch clashed with my rough skin,
Dried petals clinging to the rose blush
But wilting beneath a cruel sun.
You loved me despite the cracked land
I sowed my future on, and the dust swirled into devils
Before your haloed eyes.
I once embraced the tallest trees,
The greenest lands, the clearest streams,
But the desert speaks my name
Like an aunt beckoning me to her favorite story.
She guides me down a barren trail
That blooms before me in ocotillo,
That rattles with scorpions and howls of coyotes,
That welcome me into a new embrace
I once deemed too dead to carry on.
If you can appreciate the beauty in the dying,
Then perhaps your love can withstand
The dry seasons of my heart when my mind
Doesn't tell her how often she's adored.

Will you sing me a song?

What shall it entail?

Sing me a song about the way the butterflies swirl through your hair when the wind grabs it just right, how they tickle your nose flying too close, never sensing you as anything other than a short tree for them to land and rest.

Sing me a song about how the sunlight changes your eyes into a myriad of wildflower fields, flecks of yellow amid the brown landscape of winter, brought back to life by spring, warmth, and home.

Sing me a song about the rain catching your mustache and rolling down your lips as you lean in to kiss me, how the rain cleanses me physically as you cleanse me spiritually, drawing me back to my safety net and best friend.

Sing me a song about all the antics you perform to see me smile when your presence alone lights my soul on fire, and the lightest touch of your fingertips on my skin sends chills down my spine akin to a thousand blizzards.

Sing me a song about how you created everything from nothing when you looked at me and decided you'd be the only one to never let me go.

If my fingers were but pens

If my fingers were but pens
And your breath but ink,
Then I would write your soul a poem
And transcribe your body into a collection
Of every hope, dream, and aspiration
That ever drowned my inner critic
Because there is no greater manuscript
Than the story your energy
Carves out of mine.

Words Left Unsaid

I love you.

Words I Should Have Said

If the world ended today,
I would spend it in your arms
And feel the burn of the end
As fiercely as I felt the heat
Emanating from your touch.

How can I find someone like you?

-words left unsaid after 'I love you'

Sunset

The sun could rise a thousand ways
And set a thousand more
In colors so vibrant they aren't yet found
On an artist's board,
And still my back alone would watch
The hues reshape the skies
As my heart consumed every ounce of love
That lit up in your eyes.

"How many times can one person fall in love?"
I heard you smile in the dark.
"How many lives do you plan on living?"

Would a rose by any other name speak to me
Like fireflies guiding me into a darkened wood
To anguish beneath the tortured screams
Of all the people I failed to love correctly?
Is there such a thing as endless love, or do we reshare
The abundance shoved upon us by others, and that's why
We're all broken? I ran out of love for myself;
Now I only share fragments of love I found off the curb.
I emptied the well of love from my dearest companions;
Now I hoard the love I told myself I deserved,
The kind, gentle, warm love that I realized was more sparse
Than the clean waters in the oceans. Take me to the rose that
Strikes me with its petals, soothes me
With its thorns, and I will find my tattered peace.

Hearts are fragile, little things.
They break easier than glass.
But my heart beats with the strength
Of a thousand horses galloping
Across the Texas plains
When it hears your voice.
A muscle that pulses with life
When your fingertips graze my flesh
Hammers outside of my chest,
And it takes all my effort to catch it.
I will cherish you until the sun dies,
Until the planet falls into its final night,
And my heart will finally rest in tandem
Beside the fragile beat of yours.

Romance is red,
Violets are blue,
And romanticism transforms them into lovers,
Into dazzling breaths of lilac, fuchsia, and lavender—
Royal on first glance but sweet on the second.
The softness of happiness is found in the grayness of mauve,
Reminding us that all is sacred
In the garden of contentment.

~~Wife~~ ~~Spouse~~ ~~Partner~~ Best Friend

I sought the wrong titles
And ran headfirst into heartbreak.
The futures I believed were my birthright
Were given to women in the wings.
It wasn't until I sought the person I needed
That the titles I failed to find suddenly gathered
In generous array at my feet alongside the man
Who couldn't imagine a wife, a spouse, a partner
Who he wouldn't first think of as his best friend.

A Love Poem

With every rising day, the frailty
Of literature whispers to me. For all
The poetry written before my time
And all the poetry yet to be penned
Failed then and will fail now
To encapsulate the well of love
I filled for you. How can I
Consider myself a poet
When words alone can never do?

My beloved wraps me in cozy autumn afternoons
And smells of cinnamon, hot cocoa, and pine.
My beloved is more than the one I wed
And to the one I vowed my future
Because he didn't question my past
And only wanted my present.
My beloved breathes new life into my chest
When the world steals my breath away.
When I run from everyone and everything
To hide in a makeshift treehouse in the backyard
Amongst trumpet vines, bees, and muddy pawprints,
My beloved seeks me with nothing
But his fingertip brush of longing.
No blanket captures the comfort
He provides when he holds me tightly
And reminds me that he'd burn civilization to the ground
If it stopped one more tear from falling.

And we were yellow

Shades of gray marred my touch
Until your yellow energy cast a blush
Across my blue cheeks and pink lips.
From our hearts you conjured a new genesis,
And I ached as I clung to forgotten promises.
How long until you bore of my tiredness?
How long before your wildness
Tosses my safety net to the wayside?
Nothing to do with my time but bide
Even when you shook off the dust
And cleansed my hardened heart of rust.
Yellow surged into my soul, warm and soft,
Embraced until you melted the cold of my frost,
And the touch of your hands on mine
Brought me back to life.
Oranges, lilacs, azures, and emeralds
Heralded in a new age of love that speckled
My world in the brightest yellow sunshine.

The diamond crisis of Africa shines brightly here.
The jewelry shops rush to adorn buyers in a colorless gem
That offers no complexities and no value
Outside of what we bestow it. I always preferred pearls.
Something about the way they glisten in opaque shades
Of white, pink, gray, and blue drew me in,
A washed-up siren claiming her victim.
But it's not about the stone on the ring on my finger.
The movies build up to extravagant parties and tall cakes
And guest lists longer than a thesis paper, but what next?
The genre shifts from romance to contemporary,
Sometimes comedy, sometimes drama, but romance is gone.
How can we blame new generations for leaving marriage,
Or avoiding the institution altogether,
When we never explained how to make them work?
Anyone can love you, but not everyone can cherish you.
Anyone can love you, but not everyone will forgive you.
And you won't forgive everyone. It's our nature,
But you must find the one whom you can forgive
Because you chose to love them in everything.
The stone on my wedding band only dictated my fashion,
The dress in my photos only dictated the times,
And the new name on my license only dictates a dozen calls
To government agencies with better things to do.
But the marriage, the lifetime, and the commitment
Are as ever changing as ourselves. The true woes of
Matrimony are believing it will end a chapter of your life
Instead of enriching your journey
With your favorite companion.

I Know

When the day is too much,
I collapse beside you,
Wrap your arms around my neck,
And listen to your heartbeat until
It syncs with mine, and I know
That you are my love.

What is romance and how do I grow it?

Touched by a fuchsia petal late in the evening,
Stepping across the stones like a forbidden dance,
Swaying with the breeze as the leaves fall
In a funnel around my body,
I am met with the comforting breath of the energy
From which I was formed and to which calls me back.
The goosebumps radiating down my bare skin
Remind me of spring and autumn in one swoop—
The touch of a childhood crush and the kiss
Of a forty-seven-year marriage enveloped me
Within a floral musk flooding my senses.
I taste the pollen, I scratch the stems, I hear their murmurs
Of delicate pleas to return home and never leave.
But how can I appreciate the throes of belonging
Without giving up the freedom of the wild?
As a child, I believed I was broken
Because I preferred tea and books and softness,
But as an aged woman trapped in a body
Decaying too slowly for my mind,
I discover the secrets buried in my
Bones screaming to release.
I created romance before I knew
The word in relation to the dirt under my nails
And the sunset piercing my gaze.
The gentle hum of solace uncovers memories
Forgotten by those before me.
I give them life with my breath,
And they breathe new life into my lungs.

Wordsmith

Pixelated Memories

My grandparents cherished photographs
In black and white and shadows galore.
My parents hung sepia-toned pictures
From their childhood in alligator creeks
And cacti-covered autumns.
I remember my youth in pixels,
Muted colors in a sea of geometry
Resembling human figures through sharp-edged blocks.
I cling to the pixelated memories of summer break
Where my brother and I spent that first week
Glued to the television, consoles, and controllers
That we greased with potato chips and chicken nuggets.
We platformed our way to victory
And sowed fields of crops and trees.
We fought enemies with giant keys
And defended the keep from dragons.
We drank toilet water for radioactive science
And caught them all ten times over.
I immersed myself in the stories of my time,
Pixelated and papered, whole worlds in my hand,
And hardly enough summer to explore them all.

The smell of ink at 4:00 a.m. wakes me up as quickly as a cup of coffee with 2% milk. The black stains on my fingers required numerous cycles of soap and warm water to clean, and years after we stopped delivering newspapers could I finally believe the final drop of ink found its way out of the pores of my youth.

I remember the fall of paper and the rise of screens. I remember looking at Atlas maps at the corner store gas stations and how my aunt stopped every few hundred miles to check we were heading in the right direction on a two-day long road trip before TomTom infiltrated our cars. I remember smelling new books before I read them because the newness made me feel alive in a way my e-reader never could.

Paper and ink have never been new concepts to me, but the novelty of them now brings on harsher waves of nostalgia. Ocean waves can't compete with the desire to touch a newspaper and read the local section and find a name I recognized from school. I fantasized about being interviewed by the *Star-Telegram* and seeing my name and book cover in the muted colors of a full-page spread. I wondered what it would be like to edit articles from an overcrowded cubicle surrounded by plaques and other paper-obsessed fiends.

The ink stains reminded me that there was a world out there, one I lived in but wasn't necessarily a part of, but those ink blotches sewed me into them. A quilted blanket of humans reaching out for each other in the only physical way we could from miles apart.

We delivered the local newspaper from when I turned eight until I was twenty-one. I nearly started and ended my schooling with the work, but it wasn't work until I hit my teens and realized other kids didn't wake up and go to work with their parents before school started. But they also didn't have 4:00 a.m. talks with their moms about politics, social issues, and health that fundamentally shaped the kinds of adults they'd become. The working class may not look the same as it did 100 years ago, but the people do: we're the ones above surviving but just below thriving, and working comes as second nature to us as breathing.

I don't miss the early mornings and the daily output, but I miss the smell of ink filling the car and the paper between my fingers and bundling up during the winter while the windows stayed down and blasted me with frigid air. I miss the parts of childhood that perhaps wasn't meant for a child, but I found adventure in the late-night drives and seeing the town through faded fog lights.

Between 4:00 a.m. and 5:00 a.m. the world is a little different, and I can't help but reminisce when I was once a phantom on the road, wondering what the sleeping residents I passed dreamt of while I passed in the night.

Ode to Art of Espresso

I sipped on white and dark hot chocolates
And played board games by the window.
I devoured blondies with macadamia nuts
And relished that a food was named after me.
My mother loved the pink and purple bras
Decorating the tree out front and shared the anger
At those complaints aimed at the owner
Without understanding the importance
Of pink bras throughout the month of October.
I never remembered that kind woman's name,
But the chocolate and sweets still dance on my tongue
More than two decades after I last stepped foot
In the last great coffee shop of Eastchase.

Reading dictionaries

I spent most of my childhood believing
That 'collaq.' was a word of its own
Instead of understanding it as merely
An abbreviation for colloquial. Now I
Annoy my conversationalist partners
By sprinkling archaic terms amid
The mundane choices of their vernacular,
And it's in my advanced colloquialism
That I smile at the memory of eleven-
Year-old me reading the dictionary
So I could learn new words for the
Commonplace, ordinary, everyday.

Don't be like the others
Who forged the way for you.
Don't only praise them in sleep
Because their faces blur and
You can't recall their names
From the vices that stole them.
Don't dive into drugs and liquor
Because you're so distraught that nothing
Makes you feel more alive than teetering
On the precipice of death.
Who are you to judge their pain?
They wrote to heal their trauma,
They wrote to share their grief,
They wrote to comfort others who never
Spoke a word of their abuse
Because of the backlash they would receive
Speaking to the likes of heartless like you.
We write because nothing else helps,
So do not let judgment slip from your lips
As if to backhand compliment my comrades.
I aim to transform into whatever mad
Concoction of poise and flippancy their spirits
Allow, and if my writing is but a whisper
Of the sagas they transcribed,
Your fruitless remarks will die
On a hill of our design.

Drive a nail through my skull.
What started as a phase
Became my sole identity.

-Becoming an artist

I wrote my first poem to reassess my thoughts,
I penned the second poem to say goodbye to regrets,
And I finally breathed my third poem into life
With the inner fears of the child I buried alongside my own,
Deep in a grave no one could touch because my organs
Were the coffin and my blood was the dirt
And my decaying skin grew over it like grass
Until the world forgot the land had ever been a cemetery.
I feared the poetry would dry up like my ambitions,
But with each word that flew from my fingers,
Two more took its place, more lyrical than the former
And deeper in retrospection than a lens on the past.
With each fear I let loose into the universe,
My body finds a new wound that never healed,
A fracture that must be rebroken to repair it correctly,
So it won't cause new aches from small pricks of words
That should never hold more power than the ones I
Had never dared before to utter.

My courses in school consisted of capitalized letters
To signify I possessed a capacity for learning
That half my peers could not fathom, which led
Half my peers to resent me and the other half
To see me as their competition to please our
Underpaid instructors and overworked parents.
Intelligence is only valued if it's measured on
Fragile paper that must be kept behind glass and
Framed in wood more costly than our dining
Room table, long since missing its extra leaf.
Those diplomas, these certificates, the pieces of
Paper that prove we regurgitated enough knowledge
To accrue mountains of debt in tiny desks among peeled-
Painted rooms to spend our lives gathering more
Liabilities within yellowing wallpapered offices
Are the papers that earn us respect. My intelligence
Dwindled with each passing year because no one
Cares about what you know or what you've discovered
If it doesn't value their ambitions to earn more to
Spend more to kill the poor and the planet.
Perhaps that's why all the great languages perished.
Once a system reaches enlightenment, its people
Value other people too much, and the whole economy
Collapses because kindness may be worth its weight
In gold, but what good does that do us when even gold
Will be outweighed by digital currency we'll never hold?

Learning to embrace writing as a woman stems from a need to be accepted as a human being capable of thought. So many critics have set arbitrary rules and regulations regarding writing, specifically poetry, believing that the writers of the 1800s figured out the secret code to written success.

However, I argue that those writers simply wrote their lines and prose as influenced by the writers of the 1500s, who then wrote according to inspiration of writers from the 1300s. So on and so forth, in an endless search for a voice individual but deserving of the title, author.

The modern poetry movement is no more damaging to the written word than rock and roll was to music or post-modernism was to art. If we do not chase the newness of a style and generation, we risk losing their focus and interest. What use is poetry if no one is around to pick up a book and turn the pages? Poetry is the true spoken word of literature and thus must adapt to the changing climates of its audience.

I respect the poets of the past as much as I admire and share bread with those writing today. I hope that future writers will pen new poems in their new voices and bring to light a new movement. Art without change is neglect. Art requires nurturing, and there is nothing grand about refusing to let life bloom.

One may believe my writing is too direct, but I believe theirs is too otiose for this landscape. There has already been a Plath, an Angelou, an Akhmatova, a Dickinson. The world doesn't need a replica of them for no one will live up to their voices. However, we can read them each sunrise and create our own works of art to provide the readers of today with new poems and stories to sink their teeth into, all before sundown.

My poetry does not need to find acceptance by those sitting on boards finding words so grandiose a Middle-English dictionary is required to translate it. My words are for those breathing right now, and I will provide my experiences and craft them with our words of the here and now.

If it happened yesterday,
It never happened at all.
What will happen tomorrow
If we don't cause the domino
To fall just...
                    so...
To create the ripple
That ensures the course of action
We need for better control?
Forgive my questioning, I'm only
A writer with meager education
Of human rights and ethical business,
Neither of which is of concern
To the monopolies we traded for
Community and outreach. Reach out
For help, and the mouth that bites your hand
Will take more than the flesh.
I should know. I type with robotic fingers
And speak from a preprogrammed mouth,
And the scar that runs along the back of my neck
Was not from the chip they implanted in my head
When I refused to write happy stories.
The past didn't happen,
And neither shall the future,
For a future without its past
Is the limbo where they corral their sheep.
Have you any wool pulled over your eyes?
Or have you been so blind
You believe the eternal darkness
Is simply another long night?

On Breaking

My body craves sugar, grease, sleep,
Anything to push through the exhaustion
Of work by those who don't believe
In rest, health, and humanity.
Fires flee from my touch; the burn out
That dries out mile-high flames,
Alienates me from my work,
And silences my ears from the good words.
Please, read the stories crafted from
A bruised mind that hangs by a thread.
These delicate strings of thoughts
Stop me from careening over the edge.
When I read memoirs of broken artists,
I assumed the art drove them to madness.
But this is the new millennium, and what else
Could destroy our breath of life
More than industrialized societies
That prey on creative minds?
It's not the words that will end me,
But the inability to speak them freely.

The debate between faith and intelligence
Wars inside me like two ships in the night
Vying for the same wave, ever rising knots
That rival the wind, but how can there be
A victor when the vessel is destroyed?
My mind clings to wisdom, but my heart seeks
Wisdom in love and understanding instead of
Science and numbers. How can I be a person of
Knowledge while believing in that
Which cannot be proven?

My words bridge this gap for myself,
And I can only hope that they may help bridge
Others in their understanding, too. I have faith
In my intelligence to guide me through treacherous
Paths and to recognize those whose aim is to
Tear me down. But I possess the wisdom to understand
That I control nothing, not even my initial emotions,
And my visceral reactions even less, so how could I
Not believe that someone else is protecting me
When I'm too exhausted to protect myself?

The Next Chapter

To spend all my childhood waiting for the next big thing
Until adulthood forced me to reclaim the youth I neglected
Was not something I had on my bingo card,
But I will turn my back on the progressive waste of space
That embraces the modernity of work without health
In a game that adds track without marking the finish line.
Instead I will embrace the womanhood that comes
When a woman enters the first decade that is truly hers
And everything great that comes with the 30s:
Confidence, empathy, and independence.
Womanhood, I've found, can only be welcomed
When it is welcomed with the romanticization
That we breathed into our childhoods, a perfume
So intoxicating that we forget what is for play
And what is for growth because the two exist
Side by side, like friendship from the womb.
The new view of life brings about a shift in artistry
That I could not have discovered
Without the anger, regret, and enlightenment
That I experienced in my 20s.
Twenty-nine faded like a mist on the water
Instead of the fireworks I expected,
And thirty stepped out of the ocean
As raw and natural as a creature of the deep.
She took my hand and took off my rose-colored hope.
She kissed my face and guided me home.

Wanderer

Our mothers were right, I'm sorry to report

They said our childhood would pass in the blink of an eye,
And unlike Santa Claus and the Tooth Fairy,
This wasn't a lie. The creative recess of my mind
Soaked in the time I spent playing games
And writing poetry that rhymed
A little too well. But I failed to process
How my body that I thrust from monkey bars
And tore apart on asphalt would one day cripple
From too many steps between home and the local park.
Yesterday I jumped, today I cracked when I stood,
And tomorrow is a fear of everything that will become
And everything that will be gone.
I entered adulthood in my body before I ever did my mind,
Blinded by dreams and aspirations
That now aspirate my lungs.
Each day I add a new urn to the shelf I built
To hold trophies for me and all my accomplishments.
I dreamt of loud parties and deafening applause,
But now I celebrate silently with ashes of family I lost.

I remember all my father taught me.
You know you've crossed the border
Between Texas and Louisiana
When the car shakes and rattles.
Gas is more expensive in Oklahoma
Because it's not full of additives.
If the country fell into anarchy,
We'd still function because our state
Is the only one with a grid powerful enough
To sustain us without external aid.
Always talk about death because that's
The only way to not be scared when it's time
To let your loved ones know it's okay to let go.
All these lessons, but I still don't know
The first thing about living outside your shadow
Without your hand to hold.

When will it end?

The orange and pink sunrise rose
The same as the previous 618 mornings,
But this dawn lingered like smog after a fire,
Unclean and hazy, desperately clinging
To the remains of its life before winds drove it away.
I wept on the drive to work,
An obligation that waned with each mile,
My brain winning the battle with my heart
Despite my blotchy cheeks and puffy eyes.
When will it end?
We celebrated your birthday with iced brownies
And skipped the whiskey this time.
Jokes that rivaled yours led to sore cheeks
And watery eyes as the laughter flowed
Late into the evening, far later
Than I normally partake until the moon rose
And the night sky twinkled with low clouds
And faraway stars that whisper to me on soft breezes.
I ask them with a wavered breath,
When will it end?
I seek loved ones but can't speak
Of the pains that wrack my soul though I need
The touch and comfort and for them to remind me
That my grief isn't temporary.
My mind plays 8-bit games that haze
My vision and blur the colors
To where the pain of missing you
Looks like the pain I saw you in,
And I don't wish you back to that,
But I wish to hold you again
So you can let me know when this grief will end.

Grief demands to be remembered

My mother laments I don't dedicate
More words in her image,
But I can't explain in any language
How love brightens my smile,
But grief wets my pen.
Ink flows across the page like tear stains
On a funeral pamphlet,
Wrinkled and discolored from a printer
Rather than age. Grief demands
To be remembered, when love
Does not need to try. Difficulty comes
In my hazy memory of what
I heard my father say when I was a teen,
But ease is in phoning my mother
To ask if she's also forgotten
What we spoke about last week.

Growing

You watched me grow up, but won't see me
Grow old. I weave your memory into as many words
As my language allows, but still you remain
Like sand between my fingers. I feel you here,
But you slip away, belonging not
To me, but to everything and nothing.
I never wrote happy memories of my upbringing
Until I was brought up. How fickle childhood blurs
The images swimming in my head, how clear my
Vision spurs when I no longer hold onto regret.
I couldn't appreciate the greatness you were
Until death masked your errors in veils,
And now I carve your face into forever.
Forgive me. I couldn't see the truth as I grew,
But now your memory is in all I see.

Marcescent

The wounds may have healed
If I wasn't so bold
In tearing them open
To stop the cold.

Empathetic Siren

Your tears tug on my heart, but my face never betrays
The fracture rupturing in my chest when you say,
"I don't want to die, but I can't live anymore."
I know what you mean. I know what it means
To leave this plane behind and be–

                                                    nowhere.

But you can't speak of it outside these walls.
It's too close to the other idea, the one that frightens
The people who don't understand our plights.
I can't erase your problems, and I can't erase you.
But I will sing to you until you fall asleep,
Fitful with alcohol and anxiety,
And perhaps in the morning you'll feel better.
Perhaps in the morning you'll want to stay.
I understand you don't want to be here,
But please understand why I can't

                                                    go there.

Diving

Clutch your pearls, you swine, and
Enjoy the free lunch while you can.
You snuck hits on an old tree stump
The day his ashes spread.
See and see no more,
Weeping how you lost
Your golden nugget of a man,
A flesh and blood diamond!
Could you believe it, Jim?
His ghost haunts me
In a manner you can't conceive.
His phantom paints your portraits,
Good times etched in smoke
And tattered walls.
The racket of a pool hall
Reverberates in an empty bar
That dove too far underground
And readied its own grave
Deep inside musty caves.
Cemeteries, crinkled bills, and cigarettes:
The only remnants he ever left.
I hope one day he haunts you, too,
And you finally learn what I already knew.

Diving without gear
Only takes you far from here.

Self-inflicted

You say it doesn't hurt
When you mark your body.
You've done it for years,
What's one more?
But I run my fingers
Across your skin,
And you can't lie and tell me
It doesn't feel better.
Just because you're accustomed
To the pain, doesn't mean
It needs to exist.

I drove south to flee the clouds in the north,
But the wild winds found me before
My feet found the dryness of a motel floor.
I weathered the weather in the comfort
Of my car seats and their worn leather,
Musk that always smelled of whiskey and stale
Cigarette smoke that awoke your memory, the pale
Comparison to your vibrant crystal eyes
Brightening the dark, billowing skies.
No matter the distance or how fast I flew,
I never escaped the storms in the rearview.
From wishing you would leave
To begging you to stay,
Please know I always wanted you to be okay.

Define well. Define you.
Define the monstrosity we welcomed in
When we played politics like a game,
Forgetting the direct line from paper rules
To the hungry children in section eight.
I have been well, sure,
Compared to their empty belly.
They would have been fed
If the laws for marijuana weren't harsher
Than the laws for cocaine and heroin.
If her parents had gone to school
Instead of dropping out to work
To scavenge for food in a metaphorical desert.
I've been well, but I've been better, too.
How much well do you want me to be?
I'm a woman and a writer and oh so tired.
Tell me how you want me to be,
And I will find the energy needed
To give you the comforting answer you seek.

Autumnal

The call of orange leaves and early evenings
Calls to my being as a woman to her beloved.
We were birthed in the spring,
But our skin sheds the bleakness we gather
When the trees rest and the animals slumber.
Autumn summons us to her bosom
To grant us respite from the bustling world
That fails to understand how we need the fall
Like we need the air, water, and ink
To push life into our starving hearts.
We curate memorials for the start of death
For she has always been more forgiving
Than the beats that beat us down
Until we are pleasurable on their tongues
Instead of accepting the wild we embrace
As children of the harvest moon.

New Year, New Moon, New Spring

Run through the grass with me and kick off your shoes.
Taste the heat of the summer and the chill of the breeze.
Find the passion of your heart, and with your hands seize
The last piece needed to achieve your youthful dreams.
Our bodies are reborn each night we lay them to rest,
The air of our ancestors rising and lowering in our chests.
In the morning, we reclaim power over our fears.
As the year starts again, as the moon reappears,
As the first flower of spring blooms beneath our feet.
Kiss your reflection and watch her flourish.
It's a new year, a new moon, a new spring,
A new you, now, here, and forever if you wish.

Self

You will know love greater than the heavens,
Deeper than the waters of the earth,
Brighter than the sun of space,
If only you uncovered the mirrors
And finally faced yourself.

How Nature Intended

Women are compared to nature:
Fair as a summer's day, floral as a rose,
Soft as a petal, controlled by the ocean
And her sister moon. But we are not
The softest forces to walk the land.
We can only create the ideal meadow
And the tallest mountain when we aren't
Broken down and torn apart
And used as fuel for man's next conquest.
So like nature, who summons the fiercest winds
And wildest rains to correct man's mistakes,
So, too, will we women cause a rift amongst
Society and expectations and the flaws of man.
We will overthrow your unjust laws
Like the Pacific overthrows your ships,
And we will tear down your glass ceilings
Like the F5s tear down your pretty buildings.
We will fight back until we bleed, and then fight
Harder, for men could never bleed as freely
As the ones designed to create life
To carry their namesakes. We will fight
And attack and scream and destroy
Until our lives and our safety are accounted for
Once more, as nature always intended.

I ran out of memory on my last cell phone
Because I refused to stop stealing photos
Of the blue and orange landscape painted for me each night.
The swirls of pink that never resembled the cotton candy
That suffocated pop songs of my generation,
But rather the wisps of meringue when I finally
Captured the peaks and dusted the tops
With the light flame of a torch, just as the sun
Dusted the swirls dancing between the clouds.
The once chalky white clouds transformed into pastels
That I only saw in oversaturated dreams and faded neon signs.
Deep goldens, rusty purples, and burnt oranges
Wrapped in a powder blush that graced my cheeks
On the cusp of autumn on the perfect leaf-fallen day.
Films depicted these flashes of wonder as romantic
But never for a solo woman who saw its beauty as a mirror,
Radiating her inner truth and deepest breaths
As the only phenomenon deserving to kiss
The dried and worn knuckles of our hands.
We are goddesses of the transformation,
Catching sunsets in our eyes
And swallowing them into our souls.

Tell me her name

The woman you hold when you close your eyes,
Does she soothe your pain with a whisper?
Does she banish your demons because she knows
The spell to undo them like the ritual she uses
To heal you of their influence and abuse?
Tell me her name, and I can be her for you.
I will help you overcome the wars waging
In your mind, day and night, year after year.
I don't want to heal you for accolades.
I want you to be healed so you can taste
The freedom of life unhindered from nightmares
Disguised as memories of the ones who love you.
Tell me her name, and I will teach you to say it
Until it becomes so overused the effect is yours
To claim and transform. You seek shelter
While beneath a warm roof, and even the cashmere
Blanketing your legs cannot soothe the tremors.
Tell me your name. Tell me what name you prefer.
Tell me before you forget the wondrous person
You were until the world erupted, ash and debris
Across my favorite face that never deserved the scarring.

Petrichor

I unleash the unruliest thunderstorms down upon you,
But it's only because the smell of petrichor in your hair
Calms the fiend that lives for the destruction in the lightning.

I bid goodbye to the dreams of my womanhood,
Cursed by modern medicine and modern food,
Both killing me enough to keep my body alive
Despite my mind failing under the microscope.
I romanticized the idea of loving you
Before I undertook the brutality of losing you
Because to lose you would be to accept
That this life is flawed. Children die
Before they are children, and we accept it.
I can no longer hope to try
Unless I choose to end my time.
I pray you would have been tougher
Than this meek exterior I present,
But I fear you would have been too fragile
For the sharpness this society requires.
I will reframe my perspective.
I lost you because this world
Wasn't good enough for you,
And I'm sorry I haven't done more
To make it a better place.
I don't know if the resentment ever fades
For other women grieving these losses,
I don't know if the sudden strikes of grief
Will ever lull to a calmer slap,
And I don't know if I'll ever be happy
With my decision to heal my body
If it means turning away from a future
Where another takes your place.
I'm here, and I'm trying, and that's enough for me,
And I hope it's enough for you.

I followed the journey laid out by my sovereign.
I obeyed the rules assigned to me at birth.
I applied more effort than my small frame contained.
I fell so spectacularly that even the ground
Forgot to shake from the quake that erupted
When I failed to question the answers given.
I don't know if I believe in stars and constellations,
But I try to be more like Mercury and fluid like air,
Hoping it might curb the nagging stress monster
That lives in my left ear. I try to remember my dear
Twins and strike back against intended harm
Because if I should be labeled two-faced,
I should show you what the other side looks like.
I try to immerse in my monkey roots and chase humor
Like the wisdom that has been chasing you,
But you are much too quick, such a pesky runner.
But the one I could never fully embrace
Was the bright, sparkling green of an emerald,
Because how could I love a gem so single-toned
When the resin that preserves life and history
Contains more flashes of orange than a Crayola box?
My namesake may not be valued as high as your jewels,
But when the world turns to dust and your people fade,
I will remember them, and I will save their tragic end
Into a new story for the next poet to spin.

Fog rolls over the road.
How can something so penetrable
Blind me from the ground my feet
Run across? From the grass that
Sticks between my toes and the dirt
That stains the calluses on my heels?
I wandered across the world,
But I return to the plot of land
That heard my first breath as if
The birthplace plays anymore an
Important role than a spot on my
Birth certificate that only signifies
My citizenship. Humanity never demands
Paperwork and identification numbers,
But the identity with which we call ourselves.
How much more running can I do
Before my heart gives out and begs me
To accept the flaws with the kindness?
My legs do not need a title, but my mind
Cannot direct neurons without first
Knowing them by name. Tell me.
When do I forget the world's rules
And return to the natural law?
In order to find a place in this city,
I must let it go and claim myself.
Woman. Warden. Wife.
Wordsmith. Wanderer. Wisps
Of what I am that fail to paint
The full picture of who I am.
I am who I tell you I shall be,
Not the titles you bestowed upon me
To fit into your story.

Thank you for reading. If you enjoyed it, please consider leaving a review on Amazon, Goodreads, or your favorite book site because it helps new readers find my books.

Follow my writing journey on Instagram and YouTube (@ambercampbellbooks) to be the first to learn about my new projects.

If it would make your inner child squeal with joy, pursue that and that alone.

About the Author

Amber Campbell is a jack-of-all-trades in the writing world: she's worked in writing, editing, and agenting (as an intern but she won't stop talking about it) before learning publishing and marketing for her poetry collections.

When she's not meticulously weaving words into sentences, she can be found in her tiny home in Texas with her husband, fur babies, and semi-aquatic son (Golden Thread Turtle).

You can find her online @AmberCampbellBooks.